What Lasts Is The Breath

Janet Eigner

Black Swan Editions

To Judy, heart to heart
life and loss,
Grand Canyon, Soul to Soul
Janet
10/14/18

For information contact publisher:

Black Swan Editions
321 W. Cordova Road
Santa Fe, New Mexico 87505 U.S.A.
BlackSwanEditions.com

Library of Congress Control Number: 2012917635

ISBN 978-0-9835023-2-6

FIRST EDITION
Typeset in Adobe Garamond Pro
Drawings: excerpts from *Before the Fall*, India ink on paper,
Steven E. Counsell, copyright 2000
Variations on Mimbres designs by Tina Severns
Cover design, book design by Geoff Habiger, Artemesia Publishing

Date of publication: 2013

for the life and memory of
Naomi Tamar Eigner-Bybee
July 9, 1965-August 31, 2002

Pottery is their language: finding a shard is like finding a syllable.

Martha Yates Ph.D.
poet, classicist, archeologist, teacher

What lasts is the breath. Its moisture binds
all creation. When someone dies at Hopi,
and then real soon it rains or snows,
we know that spirit has returned one last time.

from a Hopi mother

Contents

Foreward

New Mexico poet, Janet Eigner, has given sixty one gifts of courage to us from her encounter with death in its unexpected partnership. Janet writes in her poem, *At Hupobi,* "It is lonely living so long past the young." She is an amazingly honest, accessible, generous poet in her days of feeling alone, bereft, drowning and gasping for a breath of understanding air.

You will recognize bravery here, bravery and endurance. These are well-crafted poems—they intuitively weave words into images that provide openings to express being left alone and yet always together when an unforeseen death demands of us to reveal and utter our deepest feelings. Here are poems created from love and loss by penetrating the darkness that might empty a weaker heart of its life-blood. It is good to cry. What lasts is the breath.

James McGrath, author of *At The Edgelessness of Light; Dreaming Invisible Voices; Speaking with Magpies; Valentines and Forgeries, Mirrors and Dragons.* Santa Fe Living Treasure, New Mexico Literary Arts Award, 2013.

. . . .

Janet Eigner's *What Lasts Is The Breath* charts a decade of a mother's grief at the loss of a beloved adult daughter. Like a kind of Demeter doggedly searching through "the long, miserable journey of days," Eigner looks everywhere for what lasts: in nature, in memory, in love and family, in the clay objects her daughter sculpted, in a grandson's face, in encounters with others who teach her a different way of carrying grief, like a Hopi friend, who says "the body is like a corn stalk/What lasts is the breath." The poems are particularly vivid in the lives and sensibilities evoked, and, just as the poems voice many difficult realities, including historical and political events, they also do not shirk from the many struggles of human feeling that follow such a loss. What returns is not the ever-mourned Persephone but a hard-won instruction for the living, that in our "gathering, preserving together," those who are left can again "taste the sweet/through the rough, bitter seed."

Rebecca Seiferle: *Wild Tongue; Bitters; The Music We Dance To; The Ripped-Out Seam.* Poet Laureate—Tucson, Arizona 2012-13; Lannan Foundation Fellow, 2004; Founder/Editor, *The Drunken Boat,* online international poetry journal.

. . . .

Introduction¹

Our daughter had been a talented ceramicist, fiddler and counselor to elders with dementia. She died at 37 of an incurable brain tumor, leaving her husband, two-year-old son, and a step-son, 14. Left her brother. Her Mexican soul-sister. Left us. And to what realm did she pass?

In the decade since our daughter's death, my poems kept arriving. My spiritual seeking had been ecumenical, including the Jewish tradition in which I was raised, taking what has deep meaning from cultural, mystical, traditional and shamanic Judaism—particularly the concept, *Tikun Olam*, a metaphor for a shattering of the vessel containing the world at its inception, leading to the belief that human purpose is that in doing good deeds, we gather the shards or sparks and restore a holy wholeness to the divine order.

Especially in the early years after her passing, I reached for any coherent ritual and knowledge from any culture that would bring me to her, that would keep my contact with her alive. The stack of my poems grew, but would have been incomplete without the primal, deeply relevant messages and rituals that arrived from many good souls and their cultures, ones that I cobbled together to address the agony of my grief. Friends, family, the balm of nature, all of these sources added to the soothing that helped my self and my family retain some semblance of life-optimism. These poems document those experiences.

After the early spring Bean Dance at the Hopi's Second Mesa, we lunched with an elder. She taught us an ancient food ritual. Another time, we visited the home of a young mother at Hopi who detailed a knowing about how our daughter still resides with us—as the woman explained, the beloved returns as moisture, rain or snow—*the moisture of breath holds all creation*. I thank both women for their trust, sharing the knowledge that became this book's title and its poem, *What Lasts Is The Breath*.

A recent visit to the indigenous Mimbres world in southwest New Mexico plunged me into a newly visceral knowledge. New Mexico Western University in Silver City has preserved a large collection of Mimbres art. The tribe's mastery of increasingly bold and accomplished pottery reminded of our daughter's progress in her ceramic craft over the years. The poem, *What Lasts Is The Breath*, describes the tribe's burial practice. An opening, named a *kill hole* by archeologists, was drilled by a sorrowing Mimbres into the bottom of a ceramic bowl, then placed over the face of the departed before burial. I realized in a powerful way, beyond intellect, that our daughter, our family, has relived some universal kinship with this extinct tribe, in the experience of our family's potter, the vanished Naomi Tamar.

Each experience of wisdom from several spiritual traditions began to coalesce as one strong metaphor about shattering, about breath and restoration —essentially about restoring wholeness. Even before these experiences were intellectually understandable, they fully fit my skin.

Praise for *What Lasts Is The Breath*

Janet Eigner calls us to a deep place, a soul level of being with the life, loving and loss of her daughter. She artfully takes us to the place created by reflective self-revelation most often only available in hindsight when one is willing to truly go to the depths of one's grief. Her intimate revelations allow us to glimpse the complexities and universal truths of love, loss, and death.
Denys Cope, RN, BSN; *Dying: A Natural Passage.*

Adelle and I were asked to participate in a *Poetsagainstthewar* reading. Adelle read your *Wearing My Daughter's Underpants to the Peace March.* Everyone loved it. I saw the person recording the reading wipe away a tear.
Jack Foley, KPFA-FM host; critic, author, poet: *Letters/Lights—Words for Adelle; Gershwin; Adrift; Visions & Affiliations: A California Literary Time Line 1940 - 2005.*

Your poetry is hauntingly and wrenchingly gripping and beautiful.
Robert Stolorow, Ph.D., Institute Contemporary Psychoanalysis; *Trauma and Human Existence.*

I have fingered so many of these words/ that now are pearls/...I am dashed against the wall of my own humanness/reading your words/ and thrown into the sea of terror/ you almost drowned in/Naomi is at peace/I pray you are too/ how beautiful this offering/dare I say it?/to the gods.
Judith Fein, playwright, screen writer, performer, travel journalist, author; *Indian Time; Life is a Trip;* blogs on: *YourLifeisaTrip; Psychology Today; Huffington Post.*

Thank you for sharing this extraordinary work wrought of the ashes of grief. It is amazing how you were able to make such a work of beauty out of your harrowing experience. I shall treasure it.
Donald Levering, *Algonquins Planted Salmon; Sweeping the Skylight; The Number of Names; Outcroppings from Navajoland; Horsetail;* NEA Fellow.

We are dazzled, powerfully moved, grateful. It is raw and moving and real and exquisitely crafted. I kept being reminded of the story of the potter who said "I am only interested in what remains after the pot has been broken."
Muriel Cohan, Assoc. Prof. of Dance, U.of Kansas; **Patrick Suzeau**, Chair, Prof. of Dance, U.of Kansas; Cohan/Suzeau Dance Duets.

Visual Artists

A selected drawing from New Mexico artist, **Steven E. Counsell's** India ink series, *Before the Fall,* pairs with each chosen poem:

Section Headings with adapted Mimbres designs by **Tina Severns,** New Mexico visual artist and potter:

The Book of Ruth and Naomi

I clasp my skirt's soft, misshapen pocket,
squeezing its heft,
hearing by phone our selfless second child,
voice slurred, ill, but no one yet knows with what—
a virus, a neurological horror,
a miasma of the emotions?

We named this second child Naomi,
but she acts like Ruth the Moabite
who clung to her mother-in-law,
whither thou goest, I will go.
And I feel more like the biblical Naomi,
a survivor wise enough to garner an annuity,
counseling Ruth to *marry the old man, Boaz,*
he will provide for us both.

No, I didn't ask her to marry
for security's sake, like I had.
She chose wedded poverty instead—
two striving artists, a child and food stamps.

Raised with clueless love that thought itself wise,
my Naomi complies with others' needs—
has swallowed her own so long
they rise like feared ghosts that haunt
or joyful phantoms that slip
through her grasp like fog.

Did I say I act more like the biblical Naomi?
I conflate the two.
Right now, I'm also Ruth—
vowing love to any length to care for my child.
Following fear that our girl will never thrive
but shred herself like barley on the threshing floor.

War Resisters' Children

Our son and daughter took up social reins early on,
their own duets of neural cells programmed
for peace, for compassion.
Outran depression—he as a child,
she as a young woman—
wrestled, won that grim pogrom,
each other's shoulder always to lean on.

Son before college to a kibbutz, to prune
and pollinate date palms—fell from a tree
onto his bottom, souvenir badge—
a backache from then on.

Daughter took her Spanish from high school
to Nicaragua, through Oxfam as a translator.
Took orders from farmers for parts lost
from threshers, combines, tractors.
When the bus driver thought *outsider*,
tried to boot her or charge double fare—
she emptied the bus full of women taking chickens
to market, and the señoras shouted, in Español,
let her on! And they won.

Son to aid Sandinista families through war.
Witnessed a rebel's funeral every day, escaped
from the country with a U.S. reporter and ulcer
just before Reagan's Contras attacked
from the border.

Daughter raising a stepson on food stamps
and minimum wage, brought health help
to immigrants plucking mushrooms
in Pennsylvania's damp farm caves.

Son after college, a conduit to welfares' poor
who would fare a modicum better in Michigan.
Daughter back to Missouri, stretched
the dementia-stricken: unfolded newsprint,
circled the wheelchairs, read the day's news,
fanned rare words of conversation.

Both fed their gifting hearts with books,
with art and song. Rode the notes of music
to their source. Played for peanuts—
old fiddle tunes for her, jazz saxophone for him.
Each with tune-tappers: she in bars, parties
in town, on gravel bars along rural white-waters;

he, with West Coast multi-color bands
and Fifties pop-song revivalists; large local gigs—
not solo but peopled in harmony. Not self-sacrificing,
these well-nourished, playful world citizens.
Shaped by our Holocaust families to *catch the fallen,
heal the sick, free the captives*...aren't these the prescripts
heard from church, mosque, temple, pagoda?

Ours heard it from the womb, on vinyl folk records,
on draft card marches, when TV crews turned up
to film us, the couple who wouldn't pay war taxes
while cameras filmed the IRS refund check—
accidentally sent us.

Our daughter-in-law once asked,
*why do all the homeless ones,
the street people, flock to your son for cash?*
The blood-scent of compassion
we won't run from or wash off.

Blackjacked

Bedtime ritual in the Pepto Bismol pink of her room:
she scooped an armful from the laundry basket—
stuffed tiger's striped fuzz, honey bear,

a diapered rubber doll with glazed blue eyes,
its jutted hands a lizard's texture—
and clambered up the mattress into bed.

As she drew herself against the maple
headboard with her load,
the mother felt a manic pulse rise.

The girl tossed them in the air—
her way to choose the doll
that landed nearest on her quilt,

the one she would cradle for the night.
Something ruthless, random in that pitch:
who would stay and which ones bounced
below her sight lines, muffled
on the oak floor—gravity's rejects.

Hysteria still rises, humorless now
as the mother imagines, over and again
Fate's Goddess ensconced on her divan,
weary grimace from the job she must keep

dealing down death cards like
the blackjack ace at Camelrock Casino,
cigar stub in her teeth

biting back her tobacco-juiced secret
the one my girl got at birth—
her deck stacked.

Rue Madder

She lectured me as we sat on the hard
corduroy of the Delft blue love seat.
She was eight, firm
and proud of herself asking
I need you to be more strict with me.
I loved her, my clean and gorgeous,
bright and organized daughter.

She was twenty
living an hour away.
I'd just gone to sleep.
Joe answered the late-night call
and offered comfort—
her cat, killed, run over by a car.
I mumbled, *tell her I'll call
morning, first thing.*

Months later
she mounted the steps to my office
pounded the door that held
its In Session sign
and when I opened up
screamed, *Dad knows nothing
about feelings but at least
he's always there when I need him*

then ran down the staircase
bounced her bottom hard
on my car's hood and strode away,
denting our family's patina,
its mother-of-angst three generations thick.
Oh my girl slowly fed me rue's bitter leaves
trying to attune my mother-ear.

Our Daughter's Wedding[2]

Pearls, nestled in the cush of her breasts,
reflect the coral succulence of her lips.
Her waist thin, pliant as a fresh flower's stem.
White the calla lily's thick leathery funnel.
White the cotton lace lapping the edge
of her Mexican wedding gown,
on loan from her rabbi cousin.

White Sunday. Sunday at noon, her friends
and Mexican sisters thread the hall—
pastel waves of *papel picado*. Sunday at 3,
a friend brushes her black hair, fluffs her veil.
Sunday at 5, the country finches, wrens,
cardinals ring the guests with garden song.

Sunday at 6, under the rose bower's white arch—
white the rabbi's streaming hair as he chants
Hebrew blessings over his guitar riffs.

Sunday at 6, their carriage arrives horse-drawn,
the top-hatted and tuxed
flea market merchant drives.

Guests hold up opaque white candles,
a comet's tail sparkling in the darkening night,
led to the village hall
by her old-timey music band's black-suited fiddler
past the neighbors' white faces,
watching from their porch steps,
past the cream white of the thousand
Chinese dogwood blooms' sharp-petaled stars.

White her tall boots, laced under the hem,
eager to waltz and hora. She radiates more light
than flesh across the barn's bright hoedown.
Pure, the stately waltz notes bowed
from the bride's and groom's fiddles, their knees
draped over the Knights of Pythia stage.

White, sweet, the taste of tangible
hope wafting through their union.
She rises, fiddles for the flushed
and circling cosmos warmed by her sun.

Clay Vessels

She put clay, her medium, through its pliant guises,
spun hunks that gained their balance on the wheel,
mastered useful pots and color-drenched glazes—
cobalt, cinnabar, viridian—a decade
throwing cups and bowls, rakued slab vessels,
glowing tea pots, conch-form fountains.

In the country studio her husband built and floored
with her ceramic tiles, she fashioned smooth
skull scenes: her Mexican sensibility,
not like the monkey on Frida's shoulder;
a frank take on death—flaunt it, show death's body.

Her first skills—clumsy, uneven, garish,
had made me uneasy.
Who would pay her for a clunky skull?
It's a phase, my husband guessed.

While the tumor grew unnoticed in her head,
while her headaches raged and her doctor
found nothing on the CAT scan without contrast—
like a blindered horse, he said *depression* and *sinus*—
she formed mermaids inside cerulean,
frontal lobe lagoons, massaged the clay

in her fingers to sea ropes coiled and glazed
grass-green, fired iridescent cerebella.

She's quoted in the Art League's journal:
how people think, how their thoughts range
interests me. The brain is a beautiful thing.

Later, I heard that another prescient artist
nudged acrylics across canvas,
painting brains the decade before death
hooked him hard in his head.

After she died, her husband boxed
the ceramics for their baby son—
a thinking legacy she left him.

Feeling her fate,
she threw not dice but clay.

Pitcher with Filtered Water

Long before the winter
when her dreadful headaches begin
I bring my daughter a pitcher like my own.
She pours the vessel's water
for her sons and husband
just as grandmothers Rivka and Anna
and mother Mae had been keepers
of the clean water for our healthy families
and back and back to Miriam's well.
A filled glass promises security, relief—
a mother and daughter across a thousand miles
joined to garner and preserve life.

A round small plastic calendar
adheres to the pitcher's side,
a colored ring of month abbreviations—
two months in which to drink the water
clean and thus green;
one month red—time to pitch the filter,
purge its unseen toxins.
From immigrants who thrived here,
I swallowed my parents' steadfast optimism—
in perpetuity, a safe landing.

Purchase this sparkling,
clear product, guarantee health.

Changing the charcoal filter
I felt inordinate and tangible safety
surpassing a talisman—

if we keep within the green grid's kingdom.
JULy, green, safe.

AUGust, and though I still change
the shaft and the vinyl vows
another month's clean-water-clear health,

for me, the filter,
forever red-etched

won't filter *denial*
won't filter *death*.

Messenger

Upside down on mesh
the full brown fur-fist hangs.
Jittery and thralled, I draw close,
examine the panting velvet,
its fine pinched nose, red web
veining each translucent ear.

Scraped off the screen door, the bat
falls ajump with panicked wings
to my Folgers Coffee tin.
I carry it to the pin oak's lowest fork
slide the creature from metalline sides.

Bellows of skin work air
like a kite's rattle, a fanned labor
as it flaps across the street, sticks
only seconds on a house gable,

and turns to face me
with the face of a child
and sails back toward me.

The air swarms, gray, viscous
as I turn and labor for home.

This is not human time. Only children,
they say, hear the bat's pitch
but I'm caught in a net,
my shriek as silent as the bat's.
I slam my front door, watch it

hunch on the next home's brick,
wings bent like infant elbows.
All day we peer out at each other,
more alike than not.

I feel the blood message,
the hieroglyphs her toe
brushes across my womb—

> *say Safety*
> *say Welcome*

writes the child
suspended head
down.

Tidy Mind

I clutched the phone
and my tidy mind pushed down
the fist of dread and panic
when I heard your unnatural
sing-songy voice.

That Yom Kippur, and the next
and the next—

I will forever inscribe myself
in the Book of Eternal Remorse—

a mother who could not afford
to hear and honor the message
in her own body's dread—
and so, my daughter, missed
being with you at your deathbed.

That Day

After my husband's phone call,
nest of wasps churning my chest,
quiet rage at the neurologist's
grave finger pointing
on the MRI to her brain tumor—
I vow on adrenaline's rush
to help her fight this scourge—
to organize hope, all I can gather
to bring to my daughter
and catch tomorrow's plane.

My husband or myself—we had debated
who would go to her first.
My practical needs override
this worry tsunami—call clients and cancel;
finish client reports, close up the house,
bank the earnings to fund the weeks
we'll care for our daughter and her family.

How the ordinary aids denial, wards off the dark news.

Call my neurologist friend
ask an hour's questions—

what's best and worst
the MRI can mean,
what tough queries for the hospital doc,
how to get her the best care.

Flee to the Farmer's Market
to garner color and health—
alternating numb and terror;
lavender sachet to freshen her pillow,
a zinnia bouquet, eggplant wild on purple's palatte
looping and swelled. All I can gather
to bring to my daughter.

How the errands foster denial, hedge against the dreadful.

In the wood mulch a friend gathers
me in her arms and soaks like cotton batting
a dollop of my agony, living a thousand miles west
from my girl's hospital bed where she lies
waiting for her brain's biopsy,
father and friends by her side.

At Savon, the sugarless gum
she requested by phone the night before—

the #2 reading glasses. She is thirsty
and never can get enough of words.
I love you, our exchange.

Goodnight sweetheart, I say.

Drive to my medical friends,
learn energy rituals to soothe away her fear
and to balance thought. A prescription
for pills in case the huge worry prevents
the nights' sleep…can't afford a cold, not now.

Lunch comfort from the Horseman's Cafe—
chicken enchilada soaked in red chile gravy,
side of guacamole,
iced tea with lemon, in styrofoam.

Pills at the drug store drive-through.
A brief case on wheels at Office Supplies
to slide my laptop through two airports,
rent the car, and on to Iowa.
Maybe outrace my dance article deadlines
during the long hospital hours.

Home and a dive for the food—

How good eats stoke my denial.

tang of orange and avocado,
poultry shreds doused in *adovada*.

I broadcast emails—
her brain tumor. Tell friends
we'll wait together for the biopsy
and aid her husband with the boys.

Emails finished
I grab the ringing phone.
Our son, voice warm,
a bit unraveled—

Mom, are you sitting down?

Street of the Dead, Teotihuacan

Stretching down the Pyramid of the Sun's
giant steps I can't maintain equilibrium
knowing my daughter's head throbs.
By phone, she's pleased we're learning
Spanish, our effort to match her fluency.
Then says she vomited—*probably the flu.*

Of the few quiet vendors
at the Pyramid to the Moon
one approaches
selling masks that frighten
with their fierce indifference.
I finger the androgynous mold,
its face glowing,
pieced like quilt work—
onyx, lapis, abalone—
oval holes for mouth and eyes—
void where the life would be.

I don't have to buy one and I do,
puzzled why I'm drawn
to embrace this ominous fear

until six weeks later—
the call from our son
who describes the gods' devouring:
*Mom, Naomi died at the hospital
sometime this afternoon.*

I remember Quetzalcoatl's terrible beauty
at the base of the pyramid
the jaguar's inexorable grinding jaws
the blood's ancient scent
the grinding vapor.

Sparks[3]

An electrical current fizzed
along my lip line
the day my daughter died
a thousand miles away.

I didn't credit the flare—
that from such a distance
she had put her mouth on mine,
one last lean-in kiss.

That afternoon, my head,
nearly numb to this tension
not knowing—would she live.

Tender muscles in my arms
clenched, unclenched
as her strong, disembodied hands
clutched deep into my flesh,

fought the grip of Azrael,
the death angel,
held to me until she tunneled
through to the next embrace of Space.

Had I known her kiss,
those subtle signs
that I was still with her,
would I have to wrestle

every sticker-weed for meaning,
scan the night heaven
for her silver trace?

I Didn't Reach Naomi

before she died,
didn't stroke her hair and hands,
exchange the last great loop
of braided voice and warmth,

wasn't prescient, that her bad headaches
would come to such swift silence.
Lying in her hospital bed
she asked for a pill to lessen the throb

after a string of friends' morning visits,
long distance chats.
She napped, her father thought,
but when the aide brought supper,

no one could rouse her
not her father, not the nurse,
not the staff
that swarmed over.

By phone, I, the invisible
opera prompter at *Orpheus and Eurydice*
begged her father, her stunned
and hesitant friends, her husband—

Please, please, circle her bed,
keep her spirit company,
kiss her hand and face for me,
brush her dark curls,

wreath our darling
in her loved songs, your prayers.
Sing the birthday song—
Esta son las Mañanitas.
Gentle her birth into the new world.

I heard them sing the Spanish songs,
the psalms she had sung. Voices telling
how much she was adored
calmed me a bit until my husband cried,

Her hand is getting cold!
and told how, that morning,
our daughter had said,
I wish my Mother was here.

How he replied,
You know she's with you,
and she said, *I know,*
but her prescient grief pierced.

The Song of Life and Death

Over the telephone from the hospital room
my husband cries
her hand is getting cold.

My heart, butchered by my absence
forms an arrow.
Lungs, crushed and shriveled
twist and string my bow

and I travel timeless—
span the thousand miles to her deathbed
to press my lips to hers, cradle her in my arms.

Stilled Life with Autopsy

I asked a tender friend,

Should I see her dissected
before the cremation?
Can I deny my tremendous need

to caress her goodbye?
I'm frightened
that I will be endlessly
haunted…

even now twisting
in the purgatory
of the absent.

Visitation

From the memorial, we plod down
the steep stairway, squeeze into the rental car.
To the home of Naomi's friend, a reception.

My relatives, a sudden surprise,
materialize over the doorstoop—
three generations familiar with loss,
small fortress of comfort, of breath.

My elegant aunt, composed and thin,
sits across the living room
from the front door, quietly says,

Don't think I'm crazy, but I just saw Naomi—
she stood in the front door, smiling, looked around.
Wore a slim peasant dress…the cloth, some sort of print—
little puffed sleeves, embroidered. Then she was gone.

Grief and fear dig deeper.
I'm the mother, ordinary, inadequate,
no special powers. I love and envy this aunt

who can pay attention, see spirit.
I've missed my daughter—
again.

A Little Lighter

The raw walk to the place of ashes and caskets
over unfamiliar sidewalks sloping down

step on...

to the Mississippi lapping and licking away
the bank's fecund soil. The tired brick wall,
rough red of two centuries past

step on a crack...

leads onto the atrium's thin carpet,
the director's subdued greeting,
the wait for the ziplock bag holding
locks of our daughter's dark auburn curls

step on a crack, you'll break...

the cardboard box holding her ashes
only a little less heavy than she,
a weight, newborn nursing on my breast.

Speaking With Night

Daughter, I gaze in your billion eyes
the white of your skin

a transformed, crystalline presence
dwelling, may you be, in silvered peace.

Outside the house, my body pains pale.
Coyotes shriek into cold night.

Your radiance invites me to course
this star-trail into your vibrance—

the only soft ground for solace—
my face

the white of milk,
the moon's dappled lea,

and my breasts
our suckled union.

Still, Life with Datura

You've been beautiful this season,
thank you, Lily Datura.
My words water the bush
that pushes up bricks next to my door
unbidden each spring,

unbidden and breathtaking in its beauty,
green shrub tall as a daughter
shading us from fierce noon sun—
lavish white moons, little lily-scented umbrellas
perfume and light our ink-black night.

Datura of potent spirit holds my yearning,
frightens my neighbor. Sal opens the screen door.
The leaves brush her face.

Sensing its power, she says,
I couldn't live with that plant. It's spooky.
She hasn't the need. Her girl lives.

All parts of Sacred Datura,
eaten, bring death,
yet the hawk moth waits
for its night-flower to bloom.
Wings drum the lily's tympanum,
quaffing its nectar for life.

No need to wait for fire's ignition—
death's mystery, the smoke that initiates.
No need to inhale.

I would be the moth for beauty
seeking my daughter
in Datura's night-gown.

Since her death, life is waking dream
taking me to her in a breath
reunited through Datura, our medium.

A Letter

I know you wish you hadn't turned
that particular page, especially
not in the cold leather chair before dawn,
hadn't read the lines leaking ravage.

You never expected to lose yourself
in the Valley of the Shadow,
to hold in your lap the limp, knotted
ropes of your life and your daughter's,
these coarse conundrums—uninviting handles
on cords that no longer pull you forward.

You who can no longer clasp and chant,
who have let slip from your fingers
too many frayed efforts,
may as well be blind.

Follow those brailled knots
back to the ashen hollow

though others tell you
death's your necessary subject,
the source of your startling power.
Find instead—

What?
The joy that has dribbled and dried
like pooled honey on kitchen tiles.
Rub those textured crystals
warm like a lamp that could bring to you

one wish
one—
strength
to write
in the half-light's glow.

Isaac, the Old Soul

We meet our daughter in Denver—
her husband has a meeting.
The last night of the visit
a dusty journey past the town's edge
to an old ranch. Almost dusk.

Below our picnic table, a deep slope
leads to meadow and paddock.
Naomi takes one hand of her son,
I the other, and we toddle downhill,
watch Isaac watch through the red cedar slats

how the equines shamble in the redolent grass,
play tag, as do we across the rough divide.
The horses whinny and nip. We chortle
and slog up the steep hill past sunset
wrapped in ordinary closeness.

The tiny boy, a year and a half,
has so taken us into his heart,
that his body stiffens

when he understands
we're not staying with him.
He says the only phrase
that fits the situation, the words
his 18-month-old brain
fastens on—

Don't…go…to work!
small voice, emphatic. But next day,
keeping to our blindered course
we drive back to Santa Fe,
shoulder our tasks
and miss that he'd also voiced
his mother's wish for the help
she couldn't dare to ask—stay!

I wouldn't let myself know
the terrible sickness she bore
would strike her down
while I fed the birds
watered the piñon, repacked,
readied our home
for the thousand miles back…to…her.

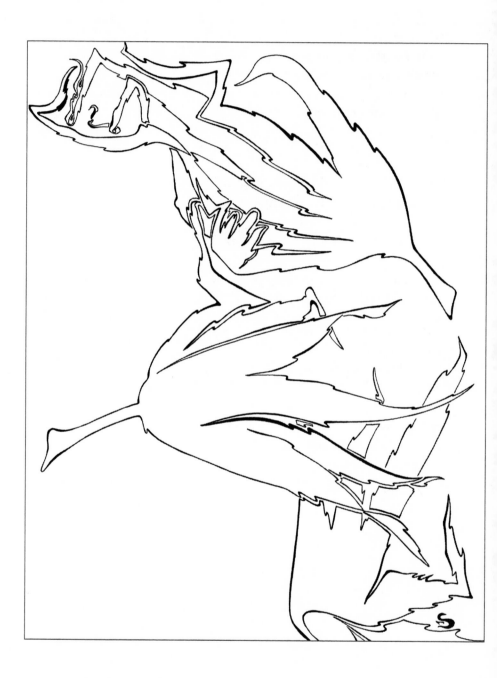

The Snake That Took Her

Three times the serpent insinuated
its glistening skin
hissed its hot snake breath—

a bold rattler, thick as my arm
and twice as long,
diamonds of red and black and white,
bold stripes on her zebra rattles
gleaming in the orchard's sun

raised her head and watched us
just after we had read our poems,
then turned and vanished, leaving
her silent, stunning trail.

A coachwhip snake
thin and adobe pink
rose up in our house
threw himself at my face
when I bent down to pin his neck

and bag him—
so close that I saw how papery skin
was starting to part from his head,
fall away,
and I saw
how he slithered like melted butter
behind the baseboard
leaving his silent, beautiful wake.

The third snake might as well have hatched
in our daughter's head.
The neurologist said no serpent,
but for days I saw it as a snake
racing along the filaments of her nerves.

What else could have so craftily hidden,
wrapped its gorgeous, muscular energy
around her brain,
dragged her to her knees,
seized and transformed
her very life
until she shed her fragile, earthly skin.

Arithmancy[4]

July, the Solar, Seventh month,
its astrology-moon in Cancer
equaled my body's pinched pain carrying her.
Three weeks late she slipped into this world.

My veins ran worry. How might I know
I'd swallowed with her challah,
the old-world, unconscious habit, superstition—
that cancer, a bad-luck tattoo would brand her.

Hadn't my cherished Romanian Gramma warned—
a cat will steal the baby's breath.
Gramma had blown three times on my baby's
clenched fist, to scare away the Evil Eye.

Seventh, July, her birth month
but the Eighth, August
seven and thirty years later
bore her away.

After she died,
we applied ourselves
to a math of the living—
her sons, our son
and his wife alive.

When the insurance man
had us fill out the long-term
care application, the number
that dissolved me was

one.

The
form's
question—

how many children?

Nearly a Husk[5]

I weep on eggs over-easy,
miss my daughter's voracious hunger,

her nibbling from my plate.
I am a cornstalk mother

husked since my daughter was plucked.
Here, Naomi, I plead,

scooping the yolk onto the plate's rim,
Ess, mein kind; eat, my child,

the words Grandma Rivka used to urge
over *mamaliga* and farm cheese.

I'm famished and desperate
for her spirit to live at my table.

Eat, my darling. My god, eat.
Mein gott, ess. Ess, mein kind.

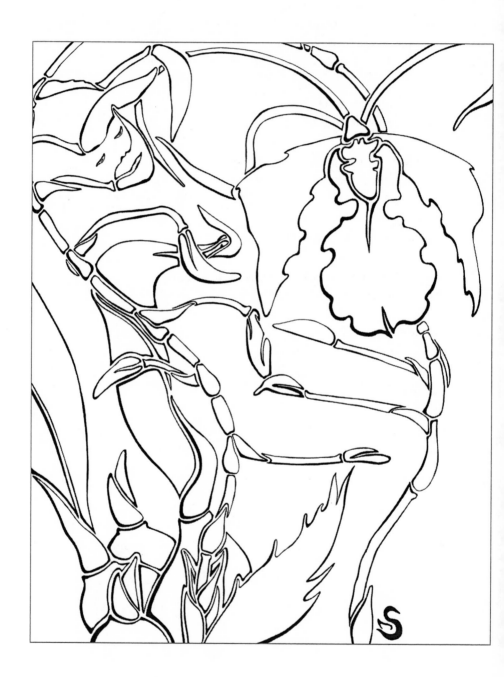

First Dream

Because I starved more than a year, nearly mad
for a dream glimpse of you, daughter,
last night, when you appeared with your brother,

I was afraid to hope and allow you in.
Asleep, I said to Adam, *Who is that?*
Both of you answered, *it's Naomi!*

Then I dared to swallow.
You wore white. Opalescent scallops
tiered your cotton wedding gown

and behind your head, luminous,
a gathering aura, saffron and tangerine,
enameling your radiance;

intense and brighter still,
a holy book's illuminated
script, circumnavigating

You, in that Light.

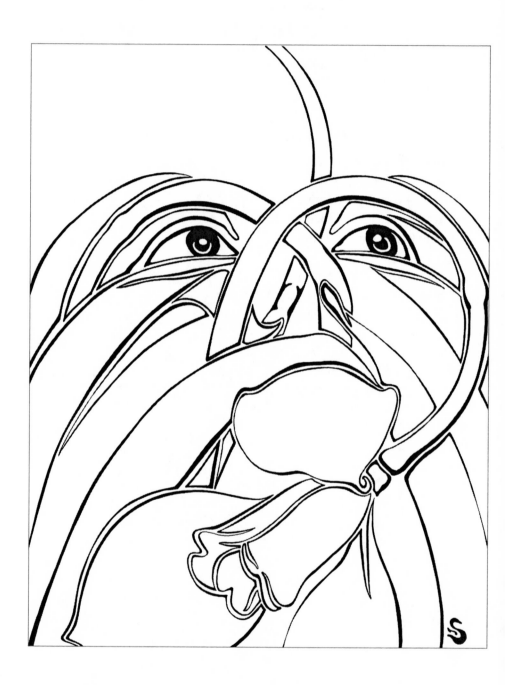

At Hupobi[6]

Where I live in the village of the one-seed juniper
by autumn the hard purple berries ripen—
sweet, resinous, they roll between my gums.

Once, I drew water and worked clay,
taught my daughter how the mirrored mica
warmed and stretched our cracking coils.
Together we placed in the fire the wet flesh
of the earth, swept off the sparkling cook pots
when the coals cooled. Like stars, the vessels
held our stew, a Milky Way foaming our corn.

She whom I bore then bore her own child,
taught that little one the clay coil song.
But when we people of Hupobi
clustered in the big boulder circle
singing the harvest spirits strong,

the vessel holding my
daughter's breath shattered.
I lift the shard to my lips.

Her little boy and his father left us,
followed the Rio Ojo south.

The cottonwoods' gold-leaf
clatters like a dry bone dance.
It is lonely living so long past the young.

Last Photo, Blue Dye

Denver, a shared evening birthday
at our cousin's crowded home.
You, among those shoulder-to-hip
at the long oak table, prop your eager son,
tell us your winter headache has lasted into spring.

Next to you, the grandmother, celebrating 89—
crone–stooped, frail—
and your toddler rounding two,
his pumping legs a little shaky on your lap
and bent over the frosted cake's

flutes and flowers, entranced
by blue dye and scarlet—florid, intense.
Eyes shining, old woman and small boy
blow on the cake's one flaming candle.

I center you three in the camera's frame.
You, a bit rumpled and distracted,
your radiance dimmed,
layered among the splash of chatter
and dishwater, the lost car keys,
kids lolling tongues,
blue-stained.

Not on Olympus

An optimistic midwife, I stand
rapt in the dark room's deep red light—
the slick paper exposed, image coming to life
in the womb of the chemical pool.

An acid-bath stops
how we family-four post exhuberant grins
on the warship USS Missouri deck,
Vietnam just ended.
Gelatin silvers our young forms, on-deck
arms fixed in raised peace vees.

Now I focus on my sole surviving
brave and smiling son
not robbed of his funny bone
by his sister's death;
our daughter-in-law, feisty and vivid;
our soul-daughter in Mexico City
nearly brought down as we
by her school sister's death;

my husband, cracked open
broken, but game and trotting
forward nevertheless.

When I turn the aperture's ring
the sharply-focused family scene—
the after-image feels wrong, raw.
Consign Olympus
to the silverware drawer.
I cannot bear
not
to see in any new configuration—
my daughter.

First *Yahrzeit*[7]

I have lost many precious items this year.
Gone, a coarse wool shawl from Cuernevaca
given by a fierce Quaker during Vietnam.

.

Sugilite necklace, three luscious strands
from Gladys at Santo Domingo—
gone, Christmas Eve while I slid through
wonder on ice in the farolitos' glow.

Gone, another shawl, deep turquoise,
fringed, woven by Muriel in Missouri
before Alzheimer's stole her mind.

Prizer of beauty, I clung to you,
my daughter—and you ran
like water through my hands.

No old ravage matches my child's death—
reenacting the loss of Naomi,
no longer expecting the shawl of constancy.

The Place of Swallows[8]

Alone, facing our plain lives,
bleak nights sobbing to sleep,

mornings quietly dying again, my husband
still living the hospital room nightmare.

We fled to old Las Golondrinas, hiked past
clear water coursing a yellowed stone mill.

Inside, Sunday-still, the clean, massive grindstone.
Up hills, over a bridge, on the back acres—

the rough log *morada* of the Penitentes.
One from the brotherhood greeted us inside.

Across the dim one-room chapel,
grimy paintings,

cottonwood *bultos* of the crucified Christ
hung from the aged wood walls.

We two Jews sat on a crude bench
along one side of the small chapel, took in,
up front, a small shrine, candles burning.

Behind the flames' grease,
the pinon's resining incense,

El Greco's color—a small painting,
the mother kneeling

arms cradling her broken son—
our hearts shattered as hers.

Aza Yoffe Donates a Life

I stumbled over the cat.
For too-long a moment
my heavy boots pressed
her neck to the floor.
Was I breaking her spine,
killing the cat I adored,
my daughter's cat who had
purred balm after her death?

    Aza on the couch, humming in my lap,
    body stretched up and spiraled,
    head and front paws
    arched over my shoulder—
    offered over grief's chasm
    one more savored detail—exactly
    how my girl had cradled her.

When the cat ran from the room
I couldn't stop wailing *Aza Yoffe,*

the Hebrew for *very well, ok, fine,*
as I searched the house,
dropped to my stomach,
found her hunched under my bed,
mouth open and pink, panting in shock,

and begged her to forgive me
for not remembering
she often shadowed me,
this generous ghost of my daughter
tripping me up—
one of her lives helping me mourn.

Before Her Gravestone Dedication

In bed the night before travel, I undulate
my sore spine against the mattress.
Between my shins, the cat, Aza, rises,
leaps to the open window-sill above our heads.

I turn and rise to my knees,
the gibbous moon in the east
silvering the feline silhouette.
We gaze, a regular search
for our girl in the cosmos.

Has she constellated with Orion,
stretched out on his side
bow drawn, levitating
above the spires of the *Cerros Negros?*

On the turnpike through Oklahoma
such a bittersweet, brief satisfaction
to finger the plastic film cylinders filled
with quarters tucked in the car door—
to control this one detail—
the trim coin stacks ready to pay the toll.

Home then, wrapped
in the desert's still comfort,
its pastel and skeletal earth,
I attack the yard weeds—
rip out an acre's prickly survivors,
fill the trailer four times,
watch the soft blue gramma grass
sprout in the bald spots, sentinels brushing
their soft auburn eyebrow tassels against my knees,
whispering, *see, you can bear the unbearable.*

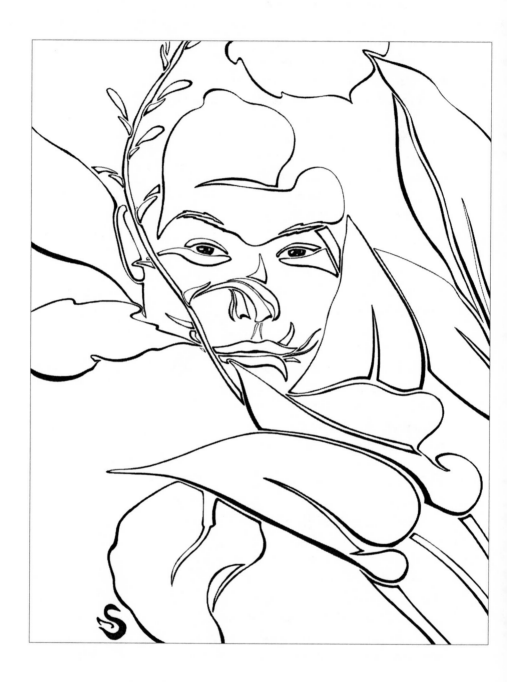

Blue Briefs

Culling my drawer of underwear
today I find the pair

I plucked from her bureau after she died,
her intact clothing already gone to Goodwill—

two unmatched socks and the panties left—
cotton, robin's egg blue and stained

with small rust spots, a small hole
near the waistband.

During the era of Vietnam,
the children were too young

to travel with us
to the peace march on Washington.

She would want to be marching today
under the cloudless southwest sky.

We'd take turns pushing her son, Isaac, in his pram,
our NO WAR sign taped to its denim roof.

I used to wake from a terrible dream.
I had lost my baby or forgotten to feed her.

Finally found, she looked shriveled, even dead.
I pull on the stained blue briefs

to feel a tangible proof of her life,
the delicious, shared hug of body and soul

that comforts both parent and child.
The dream—dried rind of her pain,

rust and ragged tear touching the decade-long
rend in the fabric of our deep affection,

even as nature's fecund texture is brutally rent—
as the world's human rhythm contracts in
fibrillation.

How in this sick and warring world
could I have imagined

it was just about us,
that nightmare's affliction?

After Birth

Three years my sorrow hangs
like concrete sacks,
then the constant ache contracts
from the half ton heft
to maybe a hundred pecks.

    The TV broadcasts a ten year old
    in love with her foster pup—
    innocent, all blind faith and trust,

thin like my girl, and our family
back then, unscathed.

    The dog can only stay one year.
    Mother and daughter must
    lead him back onstage,

    hand their gift's leather leash
    to a blind young woman.

    Webbed with loss and gratitude,
    they weep another kind of farewell.

    The camera lurches—
    catches a mongrel bitch birthing,
    licking the slick membranes.
    When the soft squeals of the newborns' rise
    beneath the dog's strong tongue
    prepping them for new life…

I live again my two youngsters
squatting beside their gray cat
who licked her kits into life…

how Life wrests
from each mother
its leash.

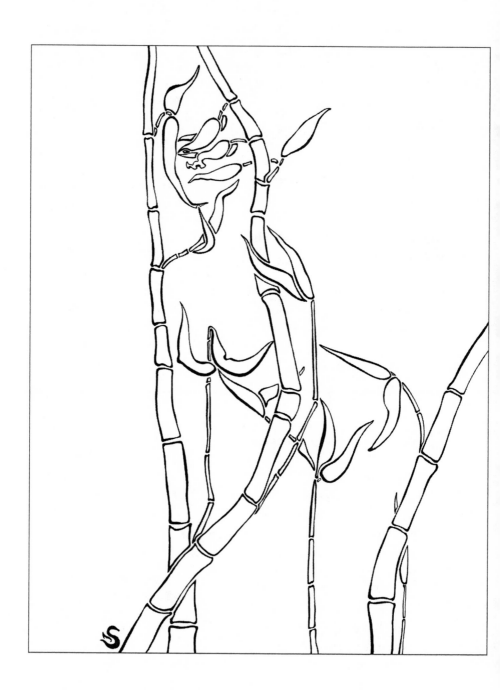

What Splits and Regenerates

Paper, Scissors, Rock—
mysterious game she watched other kids play,
never got the hang of. What did they mean,
rocks that smashed and scissors
that cut the wavering paper?

Numb, watching this Grand Canyon night,
the sky's minor constellations remain miracles
the mother can't discern.
A ghost touches her bare, sandaled foot.
Focused by fear, her Maglite
beams up a waxy, golden scorpion.
In the same instant, she squeaks,
sweeps the noncontentious scorpion far off her foot,
rises and dashes through her cabin door,

zinging with the news
that she has brushed off death's sting.
She strokes the shining mica layers that glaze the lantern.
The scorpion has refocused her well-worn
cellular vigilance.

Like the scorpion, her self split, left its shelled body. Dried.
Allowed a new, tender self to grow. And a protection—
toxin that remains to numb her.

The sheltering mica lantern sparkles.
The cabin window mirrors the flame's white-blue flicker.
Outside, poison daturas glow under the moon's wash.
Fragile mother plants may take root
too late to grow their brittle grafts—
wither, disintegrate. What splits and regenerates,
what regrows green but never regains its bloom.

Rock. Scissors. Mother. Father.

Shell. Brittle shell. *Scissors, Paper, Rock.*
Fine layers coated her girl
burgeoning with life
who shattered, disintegrated.

Rock. Scissors. Daughter.

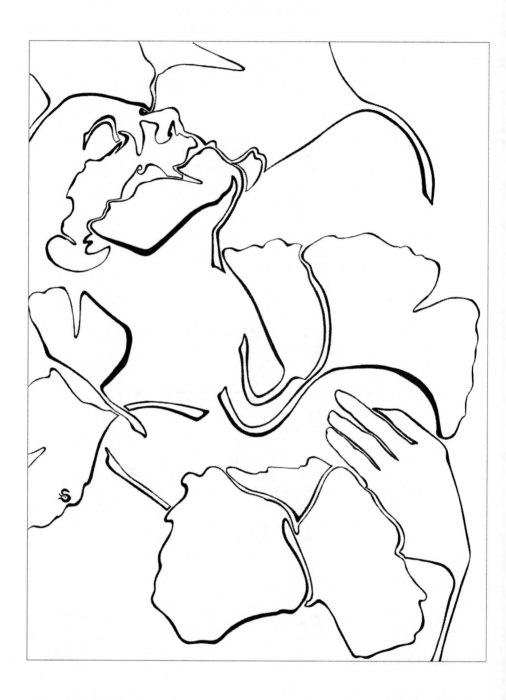

Second Yahrzeit

I light the candle for the anniversary
of our daughter's death, praying her favorite prayer—
misheberach, make our lives a blessing.

A thousand miles away, our son, too, lights a candle.
He had said, *Please don't be mad, Mom, but I wish
you and Dad had had more children back then.*

The flame glows on the stove's porcelain
and the adobe wall, even after I fling myself
like a limp, doused match, warm into deep dream.

I'm held by a man, forty, dark.
The stranger reassures,
offers a compassionate embrace.

I cling like the sweet treacle of my sleep,
draw joy to be chosen,
safe in his body's strength.

Wrung awake, I don't wonder
at his visit, balming
for those evanescent moments,

the loss.
May death for her have felt
at least this secure.

The Seed

To Naomi, on Her Birthday

Nascent sprout, after three months
you lodged hard on a nerve
at the bottom of my womb
and I knew the ache of the body
for six more months and three more weeks.
Because you counted time your own way,
I factored the sweet and the rough
like the ache of the world,

balanced, since the impossible
years you've been dead
by another muscle's deep ache—
the heart. And the wet bellows
of my lungs wheeze a caught keen.
Grief's gestation doesn't end,
lives just alter.

A page has turned.
So said my mother,
first, when I told her that our son-in-law
drove two days with our grandson
to spend a half day celebrating
Isaac's fourth birthday with our clan.

And then he finally phoned.
Do you know when blackberries are ripe?
They're green right now
in that thorn thicket behind our house.
We could make the jam together

like Naomi and Isaac and I always did.
When he asked us to save the date
from here on in,
do this gathering, preserving together,
again I could taste the sweet
through the rough, bitter seed.

Blessing Signs at Walking Stick

Two years later, I bless you,
Ali Saleh Muhammed Hussein
in Naomi's name,
sighting the terror I couldn't claim.

When I told you my dream—
a bald eagle swooped down,
plucked up a little girl,
set down in another place—

it wasn't what you said, Sufi Sheikh,
but how your jaw fell open, eyes popped wide,
the volume of air you inhaled sharply,
terror on your light-filled face.

I leave tomorrow, you said,
call me in Ramalah.
We should talk.

I didn't call.
I could never face the death of my daughter,
never face that I couldn't save her.
Had I called,
I could have been with her.

Please—
may I forgive my failure.
May my daughter forgive her mother
for not being there.

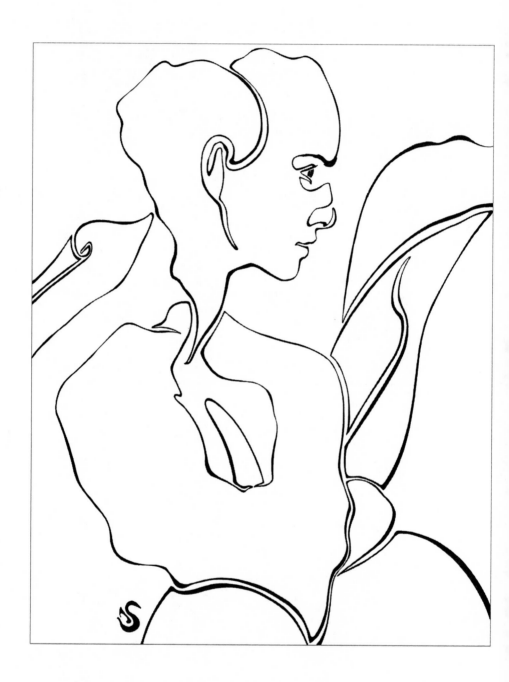

To Adam, Our Son

When you were not yet three, you asked,
Who will take care of us if you and Daddy die?
I was 23 then. You were right to wonder.

You were the one to call me years later,
ask if I was sitting down. Told me with a slow,
sad voice that Naomi had died that afternoon.

From then on, you and Evelyn—
for by then, you had married your Latin love—
became first-line supporters for us.

I can't imagine bearing the grief
without your steady phone calls, gentle inquiries—
How are you feeling, Mom; what are you and Dad up to?

Your sister's tenth yahrzeit—every year, you phone
that day, light a candle, tell stories of her
to your son. By phone, all of us sing to her
on her birthday, describe the poignant,
surprising moments we miss her, when
she's with us. You've told, *When I'm not sure*

what to do about something, Mom, I say to myself,
what would Naomi do?

On the Day of the Dead, you and Evelyn
make an altar, as do we. On yours, you put
your sister's photo, tell us by phone—avocados
and chocolate, her favorites, you've placed there.

You are joy. I could not live even half as well
without our goofy Monty Pythonesque moments,
your balm—our easy-to-live-with laughter. I can count
on your good judgment, sometimes applied,
like a skillful foot on the brake
when gravity pulls hard at us.

After her memorial service, those first tender weeks,
those hard years ago, you squared your shoulders,
looked at me clearly, to my heart's relief, said, *Mom,*
I want you to know, I'm still going to enjoy myself,
have a good life. From your wife, a soulful pledge
as she took my hands, *and I will always care for Adam.*

Neither of us could know that the question you asked
before you were three, would turn on how tenderly
you would care for us when your sister passed on.

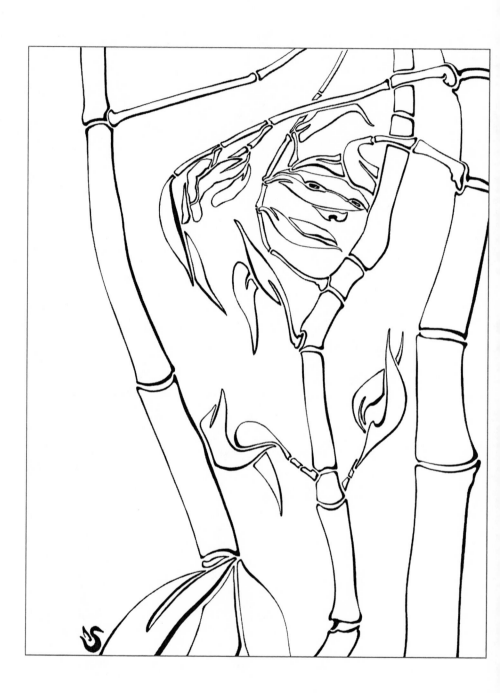

Last Harvest[9]

Isaac wobbled beside his parents on still-curved legs,
relishing the jaw and spit of green growing plants,
pitching nibbled beans into their basket.
Gramma, he'd ask over the phone,
Sing The Peas and Beans Song.
Oh it was late one night in the pale moonlight, I sang,
All the vegetables had a spree.

In late summer, our daughter,
canning green pepper,
cucumbers and corn relish,
tomatoes big as softballs,
began to sound sing-songy over the phone,
said, *My headaches are so awful.*
I'm sleeping too much.
I think there's something wrong with my brain.

As she slipped with her tiny son
into the blackberry canes,
returned with pricked fingers and berries
enough to fill a case of Mason jars for Isaac,
our worry grew.

A pathologist friend said
If she were my girl, I'd rush
her to a neurologist.

We plucked her, overripe,
on the verge of rupturing,
drove her to an emergency room.

After his mother died, Isaac wouldn't allow
the blackberry jam jars from his sight.
He ran toward us when his father tried
to bestow a jar, flexed his hands
like a cop directs traffic,
frantic and yelling, *No, no, no!*

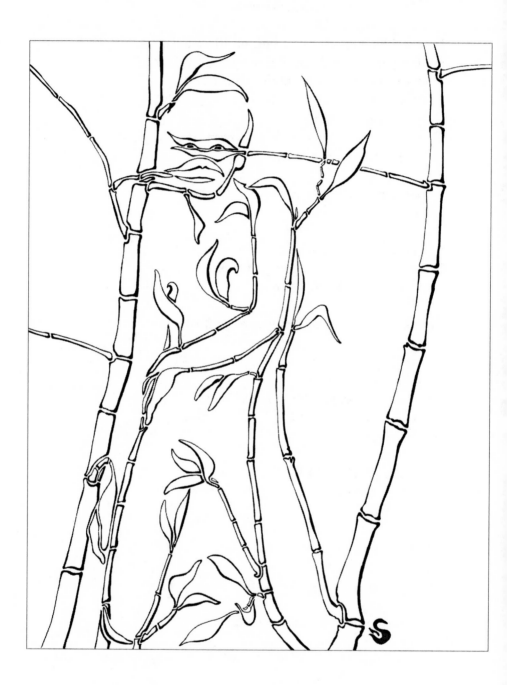

Corn Stalk Mother at Hopi[10]

Cold spring after the Hopi Bean Dance,
we stand outside the Keams Canyon Diner
with just-met Lavina from Second Mesa.
The cook hasn't shown up to open.
He's feasted and partied all the last night.
By the time he turns the key in the latch,
we're past small talk.
Lavina tells us her Hopi names.

The cook leans on a customer's table
and loudly complains—
hard luck with his car and girlfriend.
Finally food. Onto a saucer beside her plate,
Lavina places bite-sized portions—egg,
American fries, corn tortilla, bacon—

for *Maasaw*, the earth god, the death god,
whose *katsina* brings rain.
Each meal, she feeds *Maasaw's* spirit,
now that parents and husband are passed.

My heart's a sudden fit of fear
as Lavina slaps her chest, coughs.

She says, *at Hopi, we think the body is like a corn stalk.*
What lasts is the breath—its moisture holds all creation.
When someone dies and then real soon it rains or snows,
we know their spirit has returned one last time.

From her dry cough, I think Lavina, too
is turning to husk, but she says,
let's pray together, not cry.

Gramma Anna Draws Her Shades

My visiting friend
at my side as much as I allow
says, *this house is full of light and decorated
with joy that will return someday.*

A mist of Gramma Anna's old stone house
rolls in then, dim, after Aunt Hope called
from the Canal Zone, said, *Herb is gone.*
Nearly the same age our daughter died.

At eight, I don't know the waste of a man.
Hasn't Uncle Herbert already lived a lifetime?
In her hand, Gramma's soft hankie,
lavender-cologned, feels damp
since her firstborn passed on.

My Gramma Anna's heart is bad—
don't get her upset or too excited.
Still, we jump like imps on our mattresses
when she watches us on Saturday night.

Sundays, she sits on the foam doughnut
over the tan couch, waits for us,
her house next to Aunt Muddy Kohn's.
Dullll-ll-ll, loooong visits.

Weird, loud opera—alien,
from her radio console.
She says, *Richard Tucker*
you know, his father was a cantor.
Grampa Max fights with the TV boxers—

slides halfway off his easy chair, groans—
Uuh! Aah! taking the blows.
We crack peanut shells, nibble,
hold our noses—*ick*, his cigar smoke.

Now, I remember, my friend said
this house IS, not WAS, light-filled.

But I'm startled, defensive, apologetic:
I know the shades are drawn down—
my house, like Gramma's.

Itadakimasu

Each time she returned from her life in Osaka,
my sister taught us a phrase—*Itadakimasu,*
I am grateful for the gift I am receiving.

The long, miserable journey of days. What a hammock
deep love makes for us: three St. Louis graces meet
and feed us at the airport, themselves the gift. Transfer
to a small droning plane into our daughter's tiny town.
Lodge in a dark, damp motel, old New Orleans wall-
paper, French Quarter wrought iron rimming
the inside pool. Our indoor breaths of mold
and humidity feed our hearts' felt gravity.

Two memorials, one on each side
of the Mississippi. Aunt Rosalie, 81,
leg in a full cast, crawls up two flights
to the standing-room-only temple, walls
painted by our daughter and her husband.

Itadakimasu

Next day, my husband and I visit the mortuary to claim
a cardboard box holding her ashes, and one small
plastic bag holding six auburn ringlets—
hair tenderly passed to her beloveds,
the last ringlet tucked into our suitcase.

Half-day's drive to cross the river,
her burial place in our old village,
up the green hill. The rabbi who
married them a decade before
quietly chants. Cattle graze across
the rolling road. Her ashes fill
the vase she created on her wheel.

Urn touches soil in the deep hole.
Her toddler at my side bends
to his knees, eyes wild.

In the Music Hall, renovated but still pitching
slightly toward the creek—when the village
prodigies perform and the older sister plays Bach,
her slight teen face transforms, ageless. The
younger brother fiddles, recalling our girl's love
for old-timey fiddling. Then song, testimonials.
Her husband and step-son sit hunched over,
stunned, silent. For days, our next-door neighbors
feed and house friends and family. Middle of the night,
our grandson cries, *don't let them ever
take my brother to the hospital!*
Nighttime, I panic: *where's the bag with her hair?*
My son and I, flashlight to garbage, sift for the ringlet
…sob and laugh. My husband finds the bag in his valise.

Itadakimasu

A return to our desert. Old friends
care for us the first flayed weeks,
first relentless years. Sister, son, clan,
friends and our children's oldest, closest—
you breathed for us when
our daughter died. Days and weeks
and years you soothed the unspeakable.

> *Kansha Shite Imasu—*
> I am enormously thankful for your gift.
> *Arigato Gozaimashita*—Thank you so much.
> *Kansha Shite Imasu.*

Magus and Holy Child Journey the Interstate

Our daughter and he bought the Iowa farmland,
picked the blueprint and began to plan.
After she died, he soloed: a two-year-old
to raise, college students to teach,
meager salary, the new home to build alone.
In gnawing grief and bereft silence,
we waited until he could see us as family.

He cared that Isaac know his mother's side.
Mid-summer, they drove her old white Honda
past farm-black dirt to camp the Rockies,
rolled onto dust-pink mesas to stay three days.
White washcloths hung from their baseball caps—
like Midwest Bedouins surrendered to life's headwinds.

Isaac and I dug perennials—
myrrh, frankincense, lavender, pussy-toes,
his little boot driving the short shovel.
His resigned father soothed him to sleep,
warned us the boy might panic if he woke
to his only parent vanished, then left to tour
the land while we listened for our grandson.

When he awoke, his father gone,
he shrieked long, gasping for air,
until Grampa read him
Where the Wild Things Are.
Bittersweet days, a hide and seek hike
along serpentine trails, aching kisses.
I fastened him to his back-seat harness.
His father rolled Isaac's window
against an old white towel,
a caftan for the fair-skinned child.

Our two-car caravan led to the interstate.
We waved them off with leaden hearts,
watching our son-in-law slowly drive the car
around the cloverleaf, he with head up-tilted,
somber chin set, seat sharply reclined
the way she'd driven. Isaac behind him,
same side, head identically angled,
half-invisible behind the tented window.

They'd become another pair on the sad
brave trip, marking time until home
might again become bearable.

To Believe in This Living[11]

1. Cooking chili for my family, I sang
   in lonely alto moments and kitchen harmony
   with Prine spinning his story on the player,
   Make me an angel to fly from Montgomery.

   Those lyrics meant something separate
   from my own life. That burned-out woman
   needed a miracle messenger to release her life
   or bind her to this earth.

2. Sipping coffee with my friend and her mother
   whose hair, harsh strawberry blond,
   hung from her sallow lined face,
   I groped for conversation:
   Do you have other children?

   The bilious parent shot back
   I lost my daughter to kidney failure
   when she was a young mother.
   Life ain't no picnic.

   The smell of rotting resignation…
   never, I vowed, to age
   with such gall on my tongue.

3. I drink a mood-brightening tea,
   remind my lungs to breathe,
   accept the truth, my own daughter
   gone from this earth, and I

   now in sync with the futile blessing
   begged by Prine's old woman
   please, a mercy

   as if someone else could grant release
   to all who crawl with grief,
   to soar: be angels in ether.

Java and Joe

The coffee grinder's motor whines
into my dream. Its steady vibration
begins rattling doors.

Sorrow since my daughter's passing
has webbed my cells to a slow cart,
removed the bustle
that got mornings moving.
An altar in the corner
across from the bed holds
my girl's wedding photo,
a chunk of pink quartz,
the ashes of Naomi inside the ceramic vessel
that she formed on her own wheel,
a floppy sun hat, folded—she
wore that hiking the deep woods, chatting with,
jiggling her toddler in the pack on her back.

The scent of roasted beans, fractured
and dry, lying in their mine shaft,
drills its way to my pillow.
Still, I can't pry open my eyes
but listen for water's chaffy gurgle
as it navigates Mr. Coffee-Maker's tubes—

liquid licking Sumatra's berries. My dream
crawls off on scraped knees and elbows,
as slack stomach and brain quicken to the scent.
Like a raven's zephyr ride, the aroma's ribbon
threads into our room, urges my spine upright.
I angle the pillow aslant,
impatient for my spouse to appear.
I'm a guilty princess, ritually served.

The door swings open; Joseph arrives bearing
the crown jewel in its silver thermos cup.
Taste buds at attention draw
along my tongue's edge.
Opening the cup's flap, I inhale the flame
of fragrance that teases for the first sip.
Last week's coffee, like lasting sorrows,
tasted old, sharp, bitter after dental drilling,
half my mouth numbed, but each day,
as my buds awoke, java's fortune rose.
A hundred nibs dance a jig in the euphoria
that coffee brings, rolling the fluid
along my once-languid lingua.

Liquid gold returns me to my body's bedrock.
My mental detector ticks ON.

Prayer to Isaac's Great-Great-Grandmother

Tamara, my daughter named for you, left behind
a husband, a half-grown son, and a toddler.
Until Naomi Tamar died, your image
on our family photo wall mumbled *ancestor.*

Sepia-steeped, you pose, holding
your grandson, Maishe, on your lap.
Unsmiling, white hair pulled back
and bristling, you lean against the high
regal back of a carved dark settee—

daisy rosettes and acanthus leaves.
One half of your broad, smooth face
looks heroic, the other half, diminished,
grieved, your right eyelid, slumped,
strains to stay open.

Your jaw, strong and set as a boxer's,
your massive arms, muscles
sheathed in dark voile's pin-dotted delicacy.

Get away, your whole being broadcasts.
Married, but no wedding band; too weary to care,
scrubbing lentil pots that fed the waves of *shtetl* kin.
Your plain palms in the photo encircle
Maishe's hips and try to hold still
one of the little boy's hands,
blurred as a lively stifled wand.

You both look out past the camera—you
to your daughter dead in childbirth,
Maishe to the mother he will only touch
in mending dreams.
Tamara, I lost my daughter, too.

I'm on a mission to help my daughter's boy,
Isaac, laugh without his mother's joy.
Grant me your strength to see it through,
though half my face has gone sober,
the other half fierce.

My dumb love lumbers out.

Isaac's Blessing[12]

When Isaac, a small, freckled boy
approaching seven, visits us for Family Camp
he may play pirate with rubber sword;

other times he slumps in grief,
trudges along, his sacrifice and small violin
in hand, palm over his chest

saying, *mother is here*
in my heart. Before he leaves for home,
we ask if he'd like a Jewish blessing.

Our grandson's handsome face ignites.
He chirps a rousing, *yes, for a long life.*
We unfold the prayer shawl,

its Hebrew letters silvering the spring light,
hold the white *tallis* above his head,
recite the blessing in its ancient language

and then, English, adding, *for a long life.*
Isaac complains, the *tallis* didn't
touch his head, so he didn't feel the blessing.

We lower its silken ceiling
to graze his dark hair,
repeat the prayer.

The Modest Sphinx

For five years since our girl's August death,
I've shied from the summer months,
but July brings my daughter's birthnight,
and a white moth, big as a child's palm
clings vertical on the back door screen—

a silhouette, as crazed and silvered
as a moon's waxing phase,
perches until dawn.
I climb a step stool, gaze, measure
and draw the fastened creature—

its thin antennae down-folded,
short, brown and blunt, the pearled belly,
whorled and full as a finger,
tapered like a funnel,
quivering just a shade.

At dusk, the door's mesh is sparkling
with the moth's translucent eggs,
twenty seven by the next day
held like abacus beads,
each in its own wire square.

Still-raw, I wonder
in the insect-drifting moonlight.
On the third night,
when the presence washes its face
with fringed arms, slightly shifts angles
I run to books.

Io, Pamina, Atlas. I'm dizzy
as the pages fly by.
Midnight passes, moths proliferate,
Prometheus, Indian Moon, Polyphemus.
Byzantine designs, colors
lush as drenched velvets

but none as softly ashed as the one
on my summer door, until the final page—
moths the size of hummingbirds,
wings like veils a cryptic spirit might wear:
White Lined, Death's Head, Big Poplar.

Yes. *Modest Sphinx,* though the one birthing
on my door hides its hindwing's scarlet patch
beneath its forewing—
a likeness of our daughter—
humble heart, generous, bright-questing.
Even when alive, her puzzling, riddled life.

Opera Seria, Six Years Later[13]

Onstage, Rodolfo, the penniless poet, meets
Mimi, the seamstress of silk flowers,
takes her hand, sings, *Che gelida manina.*
Your tiny hand is frozen.
I grasp my husband's arm,
remember, at our girl's hospital bed
his keening, *her hand is getting cold.*

Riding *La Boheme*'s death scene
down Lethe's deathly-sweet arias,
Rodolfo clutches naive belief
that his beloved will recover—
clear as my own denial when she lay ill.

After the house lights and the music fade,
after the hall's stunned silence,
after the house reignites
and the cast materializes, links hands—
the soprano's upright radiance,
how she awakes from death—
but my girl never.
I cannot rise.

After Seven Years, Her Death Month

Consumed in the distraction of pizza,
two straws in one cup of soda bubbles,
we sit while shoppers swarm the big-box store.

Next table, another cash-trapped family,
five petite Central Americans,
handsome—such thin wrists and ankles.

The father smiles, says in good English,
from Guatemala. The mother ferries
back and forth with counter food.

Black hair gleams, like feathers of raven,
from the three lovely, lively youngsters
sharing one lemonade and two hot dogs.

Three daughters! I blot sudden hot tears
on my thin cotton sleeve, rough brown napkin,
as if to stave my loss, my daughter-hunger.

Wishbone Thanksgiving

Limp carrots swirl the pot liquor
chased by garden parsley's torpor.

Flaps of rubbery skin
coil through the current.
Below, a wish bone slips out clean.

I flail for a wish but have none, not one—
lecture myself that wishes
and hope are on order.

For six decades I've been a lively participant.
I do believe in a future
for my son and grandsons

who wiggle for best grasp
on those delicate handles.

Next time, one contestant
will crow for victory,
one will cry out of keen loss

and stretch to bear his trials
along the Universe's Spiral—

hold the short, shorn bone this time—
next, and may they be many, the winning " V."

And myself, to accept, accept
my child's early death,

suck meaning from the bone-shard
where marrow means life,
means enough.

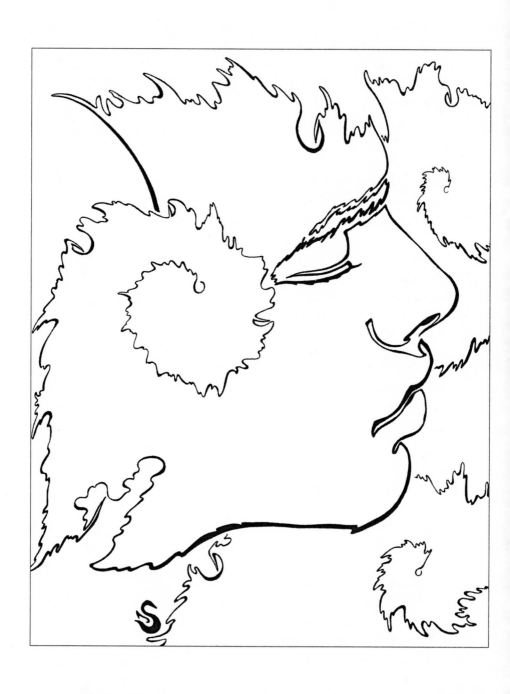

What Lasts Is the Breath

1.

Her shrine, her ashes, nestled in the vase
shaped with her own hands,
cherished in our bedroom's niche.
Marigolds, long-dried
since Dia de los Muertos,
rise from the pot's rim
with dessicated white roses.
A healing crystal, palm-size rose-quartz,
a ram's horn shofar for a joyful release
on Rosh Hashanah,
a watercolor framed in tin—
patron saint of music, Cecelia,
like Naomi at her violin,
photo of her sons, tender smiles,
Isaac in Josh's lap the year after she died,
a miniature Old Testament
bound in Yemenite filigree silver
grandparents brought for her—a joyful Jew.
The healing, Hebrew prayer, *misheberach*,
found taped to her kitchen window—
Make our lives a blessing.
Our ten years of grief absorbed
a bit into adobes' sheltering walls.

2.

At the Mimbres museum, I'm undone,
unraveled, reconfigured
by this vanished culture—gone,
like her, bold potters like her, gone,
and my own spirit whirling, drilling
deep into their world.

I am with a Mimbres mother
whose child has died.
She lifts a pot—the vessel painted inside
with her daughter's spirit animal—
scours the bottom glaze with corn cob,
water, grains, while the clan
digs up their pithouse floor,
sits the girl half-upright in her grave.

The bereaved mother, piercing the bowl,
centers a neat hole, kills the spirit of the vessel,
fits the bowl over the girl's face,
to release and transport
the daughter's spirit-exhalation.

3.

Were our dying daughter with me
and not a thousand miles distant,
had I known the Mimbres kill-bowl tradition,
for her release and to ease our agony,
our rent souls—with our own ritual tool
we would have drilled the glazed food vessel
she made for her father, killed its life,
and well after her last breath,
aided her etheric breath to pass on.

A Wheel in the Wheel[14]

By night, the melt of azure cut new tunnels
through my body—turned glacial.
A Hopi friend said the lost beloved
first returns as moisture
but I saw only drought.

On my winter birthday,
the sky's bright bowl shone lapis,
cloudless. As I dragged down the cold
graveled path toward the mail,

a tickle tendered my lips.
A column of sheer lace had dropped
from the blue as snowflakes spun
around my face, spiraled solely around me,
and the wheeling now flamed me.

A melting joy pooled certainty
that my daughter deep-swam
through some new realm,
while the great circling prairie grass
glowed dry and gold, the mountains'
juniper ridges remained wholly green.

I thanked my daughter
for her embrace,
her spirit touching
my own.

The Earth on Dialysis[15]

After the searing loss of our daughter,
we drive north—a trip to renew.
Red highway signs close in on Jasper,
warn to slow for wildlife.
By night these glowing ensigns—
antlered elk heads, silver the dark.

By day, Ice Age glaze
barely mirrors mountain peaks.
The Interglacial Highway ribbons
past a dazed doe licking asphalt.
Lines of chugging cars wait and watch.

A mountain-top tram delivers
us to a likely path for sheep.
Only one quiet survivor at the trail head
panhandles the rank tobacco stubs—
gnats buzz its rounded horns and butt.

We hike one grimy glacier's steep pitch,
gaze in fissures at swirling turquoise pools.

Axe tap by axe tap, our guide tests each inch.
Says a man slipped through an ice crack here,
traversed a tunneled chute
until, like a glistening newborn
he was birthed miles below.

Log-cabined night; I am awakened
to the strong scent of pine pitch.
On the still night air, the sound—
a brutal concussion (car and large creature)
tears at me as I lurch to clasp the comfort of you.
Then the excruciating bay of the creature,
a dirge to our narrowing,
uterine earth.

Thanksgiving, Bosque del Apache

Cranes clatter among themselves,
fly up against each other, slow motion,

float in brief dispute,
their crowns well-kissed crimson

by Gaia's roughed lips.
They land in the sanctuary like Victorian parasols,

ebony spindles in the marsh, wings like
arched umbrella spokes that prop pearl grey feathers

edged with undulating fluff.
When one crane's long sharp beak

unearths from the cornfield's stubble
a red cob with three remaining kernels—

shrunk, like your father, your brother and me,
I cry, *No, we are four*—

you, stripped of life,
present, different than before.

When the snow goose hordes rise
from the refuge ponds, and flying low

aim into the pink-streaked dawn
for the corn field rows,

their yin-yang wings tipped black, pump
muscular white breasts just over the poplars,

then my hope tips
back.

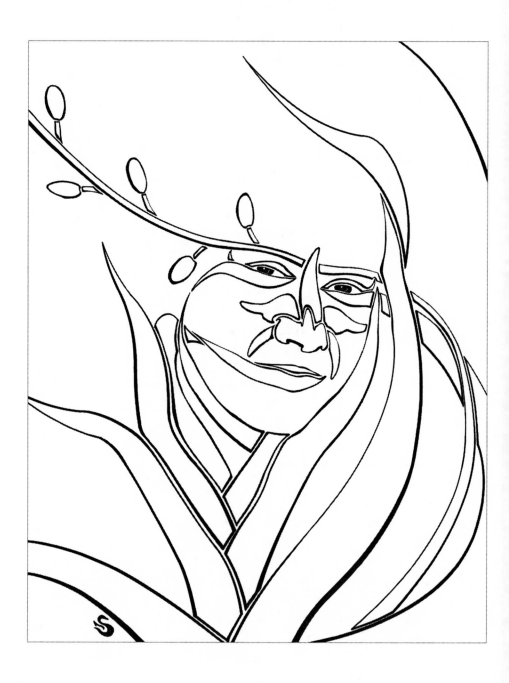

Nieto's First Voyage Forward[16]

He kicked so many months in his Mayan
mother's belly, his parents discarded the chosen
name and called him Enrique, a sound like kick,
nicknamed Quique. They added Noam
for his father's sister, the aunt,
unknown to him, three years passed on.

He rests a mere moment in his crib, flips to his belly,
assesses the pillow-wall his mother erected
along the lowered crib side, big muffins built
on the milky path from his mattress to hers.
She thinks he can't crawl forward yet,
just backward, *so don't worry.*

The infant spots my weak disguise at reading
as I softly sing, *go to sleepy*, trying not to catch his gaze,
the gleam bouncing off his cinnamon face—the spark
of the first swim in the eyes of my day-old ducklings.
He begins a painstaking siege on the wall, inching

up the pillows. He pulls still-untutored legs,
little survivalist in duck-print longjohns, arm
over chubby arm, draws himself closer, flops
his head down to rest and grins, besotted,
then draws his knees into the conspiracy—
crawls forward, spies me peeking,
my wild love—

my transformed grief careening off the bedroom walls.
The baby and I can't stop laughing
at his determined, delighted forward creep.
Like a new-born star's journey of light years
or a comet cycling back
he arrives, for now, in my lap.

Tree of Life[17]

Quique, Enrique. Enrique, Quique.
What's in your name, newborn boy?

> Enrique for your mother Evelyn's epiphany:
> your name had to sound kicky—
> how your feet danced your mama's womb—
> Enrique, Quique, Quique, Enrique.
> Parrots squawked in El Salvador,
> peeking under banana palms, as *su bisabuela*
> *y su mama Evelina,* then a *niña,* plucked feathers
> for *la sopa de pollo.* Your father, Adam, caught
> Missouri crawfish fresh from flowing rivers.
> He watched them shed their shells, fed
> Pekin ducks and boas, carried signs against war,
> climbed Israeli palms to make date trees bloom.

Enrique Noam, Enrique Noam.
What's in your name, tiny boy?

Noam for Aunt Naomi, *tante* of gentle
and generous spirit, a potter, a fiddler
whose fierce brilliance and humor
you'll only know from photos and stories.
Noam for sweetness and friendship—
the Hebrew consonants
num, eyen and *mem* shared
by Naomi and Noam.

Enrique Noam, Enrique Quique.
What's in your name, little child?

Enrique for Latino strength that surges
through Mama's Mayan branches—
El Salvador and Nicaragua.
All those fertile fingers entwine with Noam
for the Hebrew strength from your father's
tree, its trunk of grafts—
Hungarian-Lithuanian-Polish-
Russian and Romanian *zaides* and *bubbes*.
Henry, your father's maternal great-
grandfather's name, the same as yours
but in English. Energetic, bright
and enterprising ancestors, Enrique!

Enrique for *enriquecedor*: (one who enriches).
Enrique for *enriquecer*: (to enrich, to gain,
to grow rich). As your parents feed
the lives of others with their gifts—
service, kindness, earnest wisdom
and patient conversation—
so they will teach you.

Quique for all the blessings of playful,
gentle joy *su Papa y su Mama* have
to give their boy.
Quique, your feet began dancing
in utero, sparked by the salsa dance
that fired your parents' hearts.

Kick, kick, dance, if you like, Enrique.
You might dance your life.

Enrique,
Quique!

The Family Lines

This evening when a niece joins
our three-generation visit,
our six-year-old grandson's confused

whether she's a cousin or an aunt,
so I find a big tablet of newsprint and a felt tip
to pen a limb of the family tree.

When I draw two horizontal lines between
the niece's parents to show they are married,
and vertical lines beneath them

with each progeny's name, Enrique leans
close to me and the big paper pad.
He's dreamy and thoughtful.

> *Gramma Jan, I'd like to have those two lines*
> *next to my name. And I might get married*
> *or I might not.*

OK, Quique, I say, *you have time to figure that out.*
So I draw the equal sign next to his name,
leave space beyond that link.

And Gramma, he continues,
  I might want children or I might not.

OK, Quique, if you did, then
how many kids would you want?

  Maybe not any, or maybe,
  he earnestly posits, *two or four.*

Well, Quique, if you did,
how many boys, how many girls?

  Well, I might not want any,
  or maybe two boys and two girls.

And what would you name them?

He pauses long and then names the names
of four family with us in the living room.

  But Gramma,
  he continues in the sing-songy
  rhythm that binds us,
    Will you write it in pencil? I mean,
    will you write it in pencil that's erasable?

These Stunning Novels, My Elderly Aunts

When Aunt Arlene's daughter, Elyse,
a chip off the familial sparkle,
phones her mother about a dream—
her late father, Sonny, gone 6 years,
appeared with buttered milk.

Mom, says Elyse, *do you remember*
feeding us milk with butter?
Absolutely not, replies our oldest living aunt.
But, protests Elyse, *when I woke up*
I could still smell that drink.

Think about it, Mom; Dad
and the drink were so real.
All day, Arlene noodles, paces,
sifts through old menus—
mutters, *cocoa syrup, lemonade, seltzer*—
childhood treats, but not butter.

Aunt Arlene rides a starry carpet
to ethereal conversation.
Lying in bed, restless and clueless,
as dawn ascends she calls out,
Sonny, come on! You have to help!

And then words flash on the ceiling,
in RED, no less, and his voice
comes loud and cross…
OVALTINE!

Pez Globo and Tortuga Golfina[18]

The puffer fish smelled stinking dead,
washed in by the warm morning tide,
but when the grandmother knelt
by the adorable body—
not gobs of starlet-blond hair,
but platinum spikes, one inch long,
big blue eyes on either side,
fat pink lips pursed, chesty curves—
her gills still faintly moved.

They left her in a rocky pool where the Pacific
gods might decide her fate, and turned
to climb the stairway to the bungalow,
when a small brown turtle shifted in the sand.
Newly hatched and hesitant,
it plied the palm shade
with its soft paddle hands—
five strokes toward the ocean's roar,
six strokes back to shelter
near the concrete stairs.

The grandmother phoned her soul daughter,
Alejandra, who knew what to do.

When?
    After dusk or before dawn.
Until then?
    Keep it in sea water.
With a rock or sand to crawl onto?
    No. It can swim until then.
Release it where?
    In the sand, to crawl to the sea.
What's it called in the pueblo?
    Tortuga Golfina.

All day, the grandson Enrique,
her son's toddler, still shaky
on his own walking legs,
pulled himself up to the table,
peeked into the blue bucket,
squealing at the swimming baby
smaller than himself.
At dusk, they took the turtle

that Evelina had named Marina—
to the beach; trained their sights
on its slow, still-advancing, retreating efforts
through the sand. They cheered,
willing this last-to-hatch nestling to thrive,
be one not eaten among multitudes
consumed before reaching the deep sea.
By moonlight, this coin of life,
caught by one breaker,
pulled forward by another,
drawn farther, was finally waved
into what the Huicholes' call mother goddess
of the sea, *Tatei Haramara*.

Back in dry, dry Santa Fe,
Gershon the Rebbe told them,
from his synagogue
of boulders and sand—
if everything were boring as Eden,
life would be hell—
that to climb the rickety
uncertain ladder of becoming
is life's fine struggle.

White Buffalo[19]

When the twin towers fell,
I didn't feel the 3000 gone,
wrung by despair for my daughter
ten days earlier, dead of a brain tumor.

Those victims could've lived on Saturn.
Still frozen, in fragments swathed in slow
and dumb, I'd fallen away from day's time.

But when word came from Flagstaff—
the birth of a white, not albino, buffalo calf,
a 1-in-10 million occurrence
said a spokesman for Spirit Mountain Ranch,

a searing melt rose from my hooves and dropped
from my eyes, and I felt...I felt human, returned
to this time, felt one with the world's hope
and pain—how many daughters snatched
from the indigenous and peaceful, fertile lands,
and trust plucked from the earth's refugees—

Gramma Rivka's deep sighs as she tied up
a box, old clothes for Europe,
her hope already siphoned off—
like the buffalo and Buffalo People,
her Romanian sisters and a tribe nearly lost,
some still clutching the promise
that their Messiah would snatch
them from Hitler's curse.

The white calf, the newspaper wrote,
was a symbol of rebirth when the world's
people are in troubled times.

Unstoppable, some days, some nights
hope funnels through like birth
from its bubbling narrows, bursts, swells
like a glacier's azure pool and a rill of notes
from a bamboo flute…

or the dew-draped eyes
of a white calf,
its coat still slicked with birth.

Acknowledgements

Talented poets who are household names among those of us who have benefitted from their brilliance and gifted teaching, include: Jane Hirschfield at Centrum in Port Townsend, and Carolyn Forche at Split Rock in Duluth. At Washington University in St. Louis—I worked with Donald Finkel, Eric Pankey, and Jane O. Wayne. Jeanie Greensfelder, Ann Nord and I kept our peer writing group together for over a decade, all three of us working as psychologists during that time. Each of us then took a big leap to relocate our home city.

In Santa Fe, I first worked with the Calliopes of poetry, the Brigits and Minervas of creativity— Rebecca Seiferle, Judyth Hill, and Morgan Farley. In our monthly two-day workshop with Morgan, just after the loss of my daughter, poets encouraged these poems—Craig Barnes, Lonnie Howard, Enid Howarth, Frances Hunter, Jane Lipman, James McGrath, and Cynthia West. I'm grateful to each of them for their compassion and craft. Morgan called our loss a *depth charge*. And it was, and is.

My very present Calliopes include my poetic brother and sister of lesson and laughter, Steven Counsell and Jane Lipman. They have blessed these poems with close attention for a decade. For fewer years but none the less vital, my delightful companions in craft and colleageality include Blair Cooper, Elizabeth Raby, Barbara Robidoux, Judith Toler, Linda Whittenberg and Richard Wolfson.

Special gratitude to the young Hopi mother who opened her home, shared her family rituals and agreed to edit my Hopi poems for accuracy; equal gratitude to the Hopi elder at Keams Canyon who shared her food ritual. Thanks to Lynn Holm, Jane Lipman and Judith Toler for their excellent editing, deep reading and delight-filled sessions, and to Geoff Habiger for his collaborative, patient and relaxed style in a skillful final edit, book and cover design.

For the visual art in this book, gratitude also to Tina Severns, who generously shared her vivid variations on Mimbres pottery designs, keeping the extinct tribe's extraordinary aesthetic alive.

To the Apollo of artistic and poetic mythology, Steven Counsell, countless thanks for his stunning India ink drawings that match the mood and subject of many poems and provide the cover in this collection. To Hope Reed, Director of Black Swan Editions, so many thanks for her patient and skillful creation of the Black Swan Edition website and her business support, including her use of Steve's many delicious pastels to create inviting posters for our readings.

The warmth and generosity of the Santa Fe poetry community has been balm and joy. Readings at James McGrath's apple orchard, Gary Mex Glazner's Agoyo Room/Inn at Loretto, at Garcia Street Books, Dorothy Massey's Collected Works, Jim and Elizabeth Raby's evenings at the Lucky Bean, Paul White's Evenings, Argos MacCallum's Teatro Paraguas, and so many other nooks and crannies have brought many of us together, poets and friends of poetry.

Thanks to my colleagues; in friendship, these professional healers so often demonstrated their compassion—in the Dialectical Behavior Therapy group (DBT), the New Mexico Psychology Association, and the Eye Movement Desensitization Reprocessers (EMDR). The hospice and gerontology specialists who work with end-of-life issues, invited me to read these poems and facilitate their groups in sharing our experiences with loss and grief and growth, including the healing power of laughter and humor—black and otherwise.

Gratitude to my relatives and friends for whom these poems are a gift, just as they themselves have been gifts to me over our lifetimes. Thank you for bringing so much support, richness and humor into my life.

Each of you has been an enormous support in this most-challenging decade, when my parents, Mae and Leonard Benowitz, were declining in their last years of life and unable to lend support—they needed so much help themselves. I thank them for their earlier gifts—unstinting devotion, generosity, wisdom and strong example, that I drew upon to survive and grow through this loss.

For Joseph Eigner, my beloved husband for 50 years, my partner in crying and pain…and joy; so often we have melted into each others hearts and arms over the loss of our daughter. Joe has been my first editor, has supported every word and hour I've labored in the poetry vineyards, and for all of my beloveds: son, Adam, his wife, Evelyn and their son, Enrique, my sister, Judith Benowitz, brother, Martin Benowitz and wife, Jeanne, their daughter, Emily, soul daughter, Alejandra and her Rodriguez family, the Herrera family and the Bybees—John, Annette and sons Isaac and Joshua—gratitude to each of you for your lively, loving and steady presence.

Special thanks to Jennifer Bosveld, Publisher and Editor, Pudding House Publications. In 2009, she published many of these poems, in earlier versions as *Cornstalk Mother*, part of the Pudding House Chapbook Series.

Many thanks to the publishers and editors who first printed the following poems included in this collection, some in different versions:

Poetry Foundation's *American Life in Poetry*, week of April 23, 2012, Ted Kooser, former U.S. Poet Laureate and Project Director, Ed., Patricia Emile, Asst. Ed., "Isaac's Blessing."

Santa Fe Literary Review, Autumn, 2012, Miriam Sagan and Sudasi J. Clements, Eds., "Arithmancy."

Hag Sameach—Poetry for the Jewish Holidays, 2013, Gerd Stern and Judith Sokolof, Eds., *Pleasure Boat Studios*, "Isaac's Blessing."

The Daily Bleed, website, 6/1/09, "Blue Briefs," (former title: "Wearing My Daughter's Underpants to the Peace March.")

Earthships—A New Mecca Poetry Collection, 2007, Zachary Klugman and Jessica Helen Lopez, Eds., "Messenger."

Poets Against the War, website: 2/28/03, "Blue Briefs."

Manzanita Quarterly: Vol. 3, 2004, Mariah Hegarty, Ed., "Blue Briefs."

Notes

1. Introduction: A further explanation of the term *Tikun Olam* from Rabbi Gershon Winkler: "The term " *Tikun Olam*" appears as early as the eleventh century, way before Luria, for example in Rashi's commentary on the Talmud (in *Baba Mezia* 34b) &…other places in the writings of early middle-ages sages.

The Kabbalistic take on Creation: the fledgling primeval universe was completely empty, and therefore when the Light of Creation entered it, it exploded, it shattered, because it was not a "Vessel capable of grasping Blessing," having nothing within it. Shattered, it became filled with the sparks of the Light of Creation that it failed to contain, and thus, by becoming filled with something, even the debris of the implosion, it became a vessel capable of receiving the subsequent unfolding of existence as we came to know it.

Tikun Olam in the Lurianic school then evolved as a Kabbalistic concept of restoring holiness to those lost, scattered sparks through our positive actions in the world. Each time we do something positive, a few more of those shattered pieces are re-unified with the All…and more and more of the potency of the primal Divine Light of Genesis is thus restored.

In the earlier discussions of *Tikun Olam*, it boils down to the same principle sans the mystical touch, but remains about keeping things in balance through our actions and promoting harmony between one another. Same idea." **Rabbi Gershon Winkler's** email clarifications, August 26, 2012.

2. "Our Daughter's Wedding": after **Diane Wakoski's** "Blue Monday" in *Emerald Ice: Selected Poems 1962-87.*
Papel picado: cut, rectangular colored tissue paper doilies.

3. "Sparks": "The electrical fields within living cells might only be the crudest description of a vibratory process emanating from the DNA molecules composing and governing them…another meaning (of Malcut) is that within the thickest of matters is spirit; imprisoned… always ready for the renascent back to the Absolute." **Z'ev ben Shimon Halevi** *Introduction to the Cabala, Tree of Life.*

4. "Arithmancy": divination by numbers, from Greek arithmos (number) and mancy (divination).

5. "Nearly a Husk": *mamaliga,* Yiddish, Romanian corn meal mush.

6. "At Hupobi": Hupobi, a 13th-14th century pueblo village near Ojo Caliente, northern New Mexico. After a visit and a hike through this ancient dwelling place of the puebloans' ancestors, after sitting on their giant river boulders gathered around a fire pit, after lifting and fingering their pottery shards from the dry sand, I imagine what parallels my life has had to these ancients and tell the story of my daughter's death through the lens of a Hupobi elder.

7. "First Yahrzeit": (*yahr,* year, in German/Yiddish, *zeit,* time, in German/Yiddish); date of the anniversary of a death, marked with prayer and lighting of a 24 hour memorial candle.

8. "The Place of Swallows": *golondrinas,* Spanish, swallows; *morada,* Spanish, a modest cabin for Catholic prayer; *bultos,* Spanish for carved, wooden religious sculptures.

9. "Last Harvest": lyric from song Carl Martin song, "Barnyard Dance/ The Vegetable Song," 1971.

10. "Cornstalk Mother at Hopi": edits from a young mother at Hopi and quotes from her letter to the poet. All Hopi names and village locations are fictitious to protect privacy.
katsina, Spirit Being of the Hopi world.

11. "To Believe in This Living": lyric phrase from a John Prine song, "Angel From Montgomery," 1971, debut record album, *Angel From Montgomery.*

12. "Isaac's Blessing": *tallis,* Hebrew, prayer shawl.

13. "Opera Seria": Italian, serious opera.

14. "A Wheel in the Wheel": Book of Ezekiel: *The Dartmouth Bible*, The Riverside Press, 1950.

Verses 2:9-10...behold, a hand was sent unto me; and, lo, a roll of a book was therein...and there was written therein lamentations, and mourning, and woe.

Verses 1:4...behold, a whirlwind came out of the north...and a fire infolding itself, and a brightness was about it...

Verses 1:20-24...*for the spirit of the living creature was in the wheels.*

15. "The Earth on Dialysis": James Hillman's metaphor, from his Jungian workshop, "The Role of Animals in Dreams," Santa Barbara, CA.

16. "Nieto's First Voyage Forward": *nieto,* Spanish, grandson.

17. "Tree of Life": *bisabuela,* Spanish, great-grandmother;
niña, Spanish, young girl;
tante, Yiddish, aunt;
la sopa de pollo, Spanish, chicken soup;
zaide, Yiddish, grandfather.

18. "Pez Globo and Tortuga Golfina": *pez globo,* Spanish, puffer fish; *Huicholes,* indigenous tribe whose traditional territory lies in the Mexican states of Jalisco, Nayarit, Durango and Zacatecas.

19. "White Buffalo": Santa Fe NEW MEXICAN, May 2005, "Staff and wire reports."

About the Author

Janet Eigner grew up in a the small, diverse community of Michigan City, Indiana, a physical, outdoor life in the sand dunes along Lake Michigan. The beauty of rural life with dollops of urban and ethnic culture in the tri-cultural Southwest has been her nourishment.

Eigner married and raised two children while trading her performance of modern dance, for poetry and dance writing, for the Pulitzer paper in St. Louis, the Santa Fe New Mexican, Dance Magazine and Dance Critics of America. She surrendered 30 years in the private practice of psychology for more time to savor conversations with her husband of 50 years, to cook ambitious recipes with her dear friends, her grandsons and family, to support progressive politics and watch the scaled quail at her bird feeders.

The Eigners live in a semi-rural area near Santa Fe. Outside their passive solar home, they use a solar tracker for electricity, an all-electric car and very little hope that these choices will make a dent in global warming. Still, on a moment's notice, she would perform a ritual a la a Jules Feiffer cartooned modern dancer, if it would heal the earth. She and her family have lived with and loved a black dog, many ducks, a white rat with pink eyes, a boa constrictor and always a cat or two.

Her poetry is published in journals, anthologies, e-zines, and, for one shining week in 2012, on Poetry Foundation's website, *American Life in Poetry*. She's polishing tales and thoughts about her ten backpacking trips to the bottom of Grand Canyon for her next poetry book. In between, she'll be exploring horses, trails and caves with her grandsons, and baking baklava to support a Israeli-Palestinian peace camp. She reads her poetry live and on her website: www.eignerdanceswithwords.

CPSIA information can be obtained
at www.ICGtesting.com
Printed in the USA
FSOW02n2238270817
37937FS